Heartbeat of a Dreamer

Heartbeat of a Dreamer

A COLLECTION OF POEMS TO INSPIRE
AND STIR THE SOUL

MARIA TIRONE

Charleston, SC
www.PalmettoPublishing.com

Heartbeat of a Dreamer

Copyright © 2021 by Maria Tirone

All rights reserved

No portion of this book may be reproduced, stored in a retrieval system, or transmitted in any form by any means–electronic, mechanical, photocopy, recording, or other–except for brief quotations in printed reviews, without prior permission of the author.

First Edition

Hardcover ISBN: 978-1-64990-957-2

Paperback ISBN: 978-1-63837-308-7

eBook ISBN: 978-1-64990-958-9

For my lovely dreamers,

follow your heart.

Nurture your spirit.

Be yourself. Love who you are.

And *never* forget…

you are rare and beautiful!

This book is dedicated to my mom and dad,
Evelyn and Jerry.
Thank you from my heart for always
encouraging me to follow my dreams.
I love you infinitely.

Contents

Rise Up, Beautiful One 1

You Left without Saying Goodbye 5

Mystical 9

Unsung Heroes 11

Harmony 13

Yesterday's Clown 15

Road to Goodbye 17

I Met an Angel Today 19

Dreams Do Come True 23

Beloved Brother 27

I Am 29

Mountain Man 33

I Stand Accused 35

Inside My Cage 37

Hope, a Smile, and a Prayer 39

El Baile de la Vida 41

Soulmate 43

Angels of Healing	47
Self-Sabotage	51
A Love Letter to God	53
Heart of Fire and Soul	55
Why Won't You Look at Me?	57
Immeasurable Romance	59
Mama, in My Eyes	61
Over the Moon	63
I See the Beauty	65
The Silver Rose	67
Tears to Triumph	69
God's Child	71
Love Everlasting	73
Side by Side	75
Through the Pane of a Frosted Window	77
The Wind in My Soul	79
Yellow Roses for Sharon	81
What Can I Do?	83
This Poem: My Gift	85
Hollywood to Hops	89
No Color Lines	91
Mile-High Sundays	93
Who Are "They"?	95
He's a Happy Man	97
The Winter Rose	99
Smoke and Mirrors	101

Break Up	103
I Dance with God	105
Brown-Eyed Boy	107
My Brother…My Inspiration	111
Hechizado (Spellbound)	115
Torn	117
A Poem for Shea	121
You Brighten My World	123
You Are…to Me	125
Black Blood	127
You're My Everything	129
Miss Jet Set	131
In My Eyes	133
Mafia Man	135
Haunting Eyes	137
I'll Leave the Porch Light Burnin'	139
Sea of Love	141
Manic	143
Forever	145
Exposed	147
Hold onto the Fire	149

Rise Up, Beautiful One

Just yesterday, you felt intensely alive.
With an intrinsic spirit that soared to the sky
You loved…laughed…and danced,
But tonight, your heart cries for a broken romance.
Beautiful one, dry those melancholy eyes.
Secretly, you walk alone this dark night.
Shadows softly sway on the wall.
Time to pick up the pieces,
Make sense of it all.
Feeling numb, your mood, sullen and gray
You fall to your knees and pray,
For peace, tranquility
Longing to dawn a mask of anonymity.
Lost…deceived. He made you believe,
In a love…or a lie. Girl, don't you cry.
His magic spell was but a romantic tale
Whispers-tainted promises in the dark.
Empty, insignificant words by day
Run, girl, run away.

Rise up, beautiful one.
Rise up.
Let the wind carry you far from his grasp.
Rise above it all. Have the last laugh.
Hold your head high, believe in yourself.
You broke it off, put his love on a shelf.
You made the right call. He doesn't get you at all.
Rise up, beautiful one.
Rise up.
He lives in a land of make-believe.
The Hamptons…champagne and caviar,
It is all about him. What about who you are?
Rise up, beautiful one.
Rise up.
Do not look back, don't let him bring you down.
He can't steal your kingdom or your sapphire crown.
Beautiful one, stand up and fight.
Fight for the voice that he chose not to hear.
Rise up, beautiful one.
Rise up.
Your inner fire is calling you.
Close your eyes, envision yourself at your best.
That is who you really are, let go of the rest.
Time erases all things insignificant and untrue.
He doesn't deserve a treasure like you.
Has he ever been lost in your expressive eyes?

Or seen the dancing flame in pools of crystal blue?

He must be blind not to see your lovely face, or that smile.

Your thoughts are poignant, your words are wise.

With ideas so electric, they light up the sky.

Your mind is beyond his comprehension.

Did he ever pay attention?

His harsh words so careless and cruel.

The damage is done. He is such a fool.

Let the blood flow freely through your veins…

Filled with desire to live for today.

Do not stay stranded in this tempting illusion.

He will drag you down in a cloud of confusion.

He is all about himself, nothing more.

The man in the mirror is the one he adores.

Find your inner strength, begin to heal.

Only then can you find a love that is real.

This storm shall pass,

And when destiny calls…lightning will strike

The right man will come into your life.

He will see you for all that you are.

And will never leave emotional scars.

You are a work of art…

A painting, timeless…lovely…vibrant…alive.

You shine like the brightest star in the night sky.

You are a vision of beauty and grace…

A winter rose, wrapped in a blanket of velvet white.

Heartbeat of a Dreamer

Rise up, beautiful one.

On this dark, lovely night

It is time to stand up and fight.

You Left without Saying Goodbye

Well, my love, I have lost you.
I do not know where to turn. What can I do?
My shattered heart crumbles to the ground
A love like ours never again to be found.
Pain is etched deep inside me.
I lock up this agony and throw away the key.
Your passion enveloped the very flames of my heart.
Ignited by fire--pure, endless desire.
I envision your deep, hungry eyes.
I ache for the soft brush of your lips.
I am slowly sinking into the abyss.
My body aches, my head spins out of control.
The howling wind in my heart devours me whole.
I long to watch you sleep-to see you at peace.
I pray your soul to keep for eternity.
Oh, to walk with you up the black spiral staircase again,
My sweet lover, my eternal best friend,
I get lost in those starry summer nights spent with you.
Beneath the glistening light of the pale moon

Heartbeat of a Dreamer

I feel your presence in the darkness.

It is just you and me.

Alone together, our souls fly free.

My hand brushes the waves of your existence.

For the thousandth time

I would bleed just to know you are alive.

I hold you in my heart this sad lonely night.

Your breath is my breath.

Your heart is mine.

Tumultuous waves plunge me into the deep

Where lost dreams of tomorrow I will forever keep.

I hear a deafening silence echo in the night.

As I wait for the sun to rise like molasses in the sky

You left without saying goodbye.

Left me alone to cry.

I still hear your voice whisper to me.

You left behind a trail of tears in the dead-blue sea.

I long for the light of love to shine fervently again.

Life has lost all vitality and meaning.

Will this darkness ever end?

I see your smile in the clouds rolling by

In my heart you are still with me.

You will never die.

Oh, to be the air that inhabits your soul for a moment in time

Where I am yours, my love, and you are mine.

Your life flashes before me in my chaotic mind

Heartbeat of a Dreamer

I see your smile time after time.

I walk with a shackled soul, longing to be free.

I will never forget the fire between you and me.

I feel your spirit in the midnight sky.

As teardrops fall one by one from my sad, empty eyes

To lose you is the beginning of the end.

The scar on my soul will never mend.

In my heart you will forever live on

You are my sweet melody.

You are my song.

Mystical

The world is a magical playground.

My senses awakened to an array of colorful sights and echoing sounds.

I laugh with delight as I ride the merry-go-round of life.

My soul no longer filled with unrelenting darkness and strife.

Lost in a tranquil summer nights'--beauty and allure,

My emotions run deep, unequivocally pure.

I lazily gaze up at the floating stars in the mysterious sky.

I feel utterly magnificent-intensely alive.

I fly like a butterfly. I am in love with life.

Ever elusive hope no longer escapes me.

I soar like an eagle. I feel fantastically free.

I move like a wildcat through a sea of strangers,

Not feeling their icy stars, like a whimsical child without a care

Dreams of the future are intoxicatingly new,

Flights of fancy ignite in shades of orange, red, and blue.

A thousand ideas fall from the heavens in the ice blue sky.

Creativity no longer eludes me. I don't dare ask why.

I hope this euphoria never comes to an end,

The beauty of life is my long-lost friend.

Heartbeat of a Dreamer

I ache for this joy to last forever.

Possibilities are endless,

Never say never.

Unsung Heroes

This is a story of beloved soldiers.

Unsung heroes, valiant warriors

Young men filled with dreams,

Go off to battle--nothing is ever the same.

They say goodbye,

Mama cries

On her knees, she prays

"Please, God," she says, "bring my son home to me."

Childhoods lost on battlefields.

Innocence gone like yesterday's song.

Night lasts forever,

The auburn sunrise---so far away

Angels cry

Tears fall like rain from the sky,

For our soldiers lost

Unsung heroes give their all,

For the love of our country

The love of our country

Unsung heroes fight for their brothers.

Heartbeat of a Dreamer

Unsung heroes

Live and die together.

Battle cries can still be heard.

Ashes to ashes, dust to dust

Soulmates, brothers----closer than friends

Heroes until the bitter end

God bless those who leave in coffins,

Draped in stars and stripes.

A widow left to raise their children alone.

She waits for her beloved soldier to come home.

Glory to the flag that flies in red, blue, and white,

To honor our soldiers who gave up their lives.

Their legacy will live on

Now they sing with angels.

If you listen to the wind blow…

You can still hear the song,

Of unsung heroes

Unsung heroes

Harmony

This night is magic in its purest form.

As one we soar, to the heights of love's core.

We travel down a desolate road,

Far away from city lights

Surrounded by mountains in the still of the night.

No soul lingers for miles.

Harmony

Lost in our lover's hideaway,

The full moon takes my breath away.

We stretch out in the back of your flatbed,

I curl up next to you, my head sinks into your chest.

I ache to crawl inside the beat of your heart,

I would stay here forever if given the chance.

Harmony

We stare upward at the dark velvet sky.

Distant stars slowly dance.

I inch a little closer,

In love with this moment in time

Where I am yours and you are mine forever

Heartbeat of a Dreamer

Harmony

I am absorbed.

My love for you pours like a soft spring rain.

Hearts on fire

I close my eyes, drift off to sleep.

In the arms of an exquisite dream

Yesterday's Clown

He wanders the streets of Paris,
Sad clown in black and white
Tears fall from his melancholy eyes.
He hides behind a painted smile,
And lips of crimson red
Invisible to passersby
His soul of love has died.
Yesterday's clown
Had eyes to shine like stars.
He would dance beneath the silver moon,
Joy filled his rainbow heart.
Yesterday's clown
Now the crystal fire in his eyes is gone.
His dreams once full of promise
Now a long-forgotten song
Yesterday's clown
Once upon a time he waved a magic wand,
Made folks laugh and smile.
Where did he go wrong?

Heartbeat of a Dreamer

Moonbeams once danced on the streets where he performed.

The music in his heart sings no more

              Far-away dreams---too late to find,

Yesterday's clown mourns for days gone by

The crowds that once loved him now pass him by

Like he ceases to exist

Gone is his laughter---the smile no one seems to miss.

Held prisoner in a dark corner of his soul,

His ship of dreams sailed long ago.

Lost in the grace of the moonlight,

Lonely soul left to wander on one long, endless night.

Road to Goodbye

It's time to pack my clothes-it's time to go.

What tomorrow holds, hell, I don't know.

My heart bleeds, trickling on the floor,

Can't take this sorrow anymore

I know it is over, our love a forgotten song

The sweet, sweet melody is gone…gone.

Road to goodbye

I cry as I drive,

Down the long gravel road to the unknown

Leaving the farm behind. I am on my own.

Road to goodbye

We gave it our all. Babe, we tried.

We have been holding on to memories,

Happy times--long gone.

You were my sunshine; you were my rain.

The light of my life, my everything

I will miss the warmth of your smile,

And ache for your touch. I will always love you---so much.

I hear your voice-calling out to me.

I want to turn back the hands of time,

When I was yours---you were mine

This house of cards is falling fast…

Our world is crumbling. Nothing good ever lasts.

I drive on in the dark, to my destiny.

Whatever that may be.

Road to goodbye

Road to goodbye

I Met an Angel Today

(In Loving Memory of Beloved Clara Ila)

I met Angel today.

An extraordinary woman with courage and grace

Our eyes met as she passed by

Her spirit vast like the ice-blue sky

Her smile, a ray of sun that shone from within

She approached me, this natural beauty with chocolate-brown skin.

I met an Angel today.

Scenes from days gone by flashed quickly through my mind.

With joy in my heart, music in my soul

I danced in the breeze like a butterfly, free.

Until cancer brought me to my knees

This horrible disease invades…

But it cannot silence strength.

Or take away dignity, hopes, and dreams.

Within all of us who fight this fight

Lives a warrior in love with life.

A white orchid blooms in our souls

Though delicate and sweet

Its power lies in its valiant will to survive.

I met an Angel today.

Her soft voice brought me back to the moment.

"What's your name?" she smiled.

"For you I will pray."

"May I sit with you awhile?"

I met an Angel today.

Her name is Clara.

She exudes a quiet strength--understated grace

I felt a connection to her, in an indescribable way.

We talked for hours to pass the time,

She shared her story, I shared mine

We talked of injustice and tragedy in the world.

Her eyes welled up with the sadness of an innocent young girl.

I met an Angel today.

With words of wisdom that poured from her heart

She looked me square in the eyes,

Then paused, and said,

"You never know why God leads someone your way.

Like our two paths have crossed today."

Clara told me of her journey to grow closer to God.

I listened intently, holding on to every word,

Realizing I had much to learn.

I met an Angel today.

She taught me to fill each moment.

With the promise of what tomorrow may bring

Clara was called to spread love and inspiration.

A soldier for God, a sweet Angel from Heaven

She lifted my spirit with her kind presence.

And soothed my soul in a time of uncertainty and fear.

I will never forget how she gave me hope this day,

That my life was in God's hands…

And no matter the outcome, everything would be okay.

I met an Angel today.

She is lovely as a flower after a warm spring rain…

With joy and beauty as her truth

She faces adversity and pain.

Pure like the winter snow

A light emanates from her soul.

I met an Angel today.

She spoke of her grandchildren, one by one.

Her smile, bright as the noonday sun…

Her love for them flows swiftly through her veins.

Overwhelming joy written on her face.

I met an Angel today.

Clara, you made my spirit free again.

I shall never forget you, my special new friend.

I promise I will fight this battle as a warrior in pink,

And once again dare to dream.

What a blessing. You are a gift from God.

By His grace, I pray,

Our paths will cross again one day.

I met an Angel today.

Dreams Do Come True
(For Dad, Royce)

All my life, I wondered what it must be like to be the apple of your eye.

To shine like a sparkling star in the midnight sky

I wish you could have taught me to ride a bike or fly a kite.

If only I had learned about life from you

Because that's just what dads do

"Do dreams come true?"

As a little girl, I would close my eyes and envision what you are like

Strong, intelligent, kind, and wise

I pretended to have long talks with you,

With the wonder and imagination of a child

I lay on my bed---eyes shut tight,

And pictured us strolling through the forest on a starry night.

Surrounded by snowcapped mountains and whispering pines…

My senses alive, as the gentle breeze brushed my cheek.

We talked for hours, as fathers and daughters do.

You looked in my eyes and said,

"Follow your dreams. Chase them until they come true.

Have a fierce yet sweet soul--brave and tender heart, and free spirit.

Never forget that true beauty shines from within

Be true to yourself and reach for the moon.

Be fearless and conquer any storm that may come your way.

And say,"

'I am a beautiful warrior. I am at peace.

I have joy, and I am not afraid.'

Dad, your little girl is now grown. As the years swiftly rolled on,

I nearly gave up. All hope was gone.

My dream of finding you led to dead ends, and many a tear shed.

I felt sorrow in the depths of my soul.

I was incomplete. I ached to feel whole.

You crossed my mind, time after time. But what could I do?

And then it happened…my seemingly impossible dream came true

My hopes and prayers led me to you.

At last, I had a way to reach out to you.

I sat by the phone, took a deep breath, and dialed.

The sound of your voice made me smile.

You said, "Call me Dad…call me Dad."

Never in my wildest dreams would I have thought,

Three little words could bring such exhilaration and joy.

I love the effortless way our conversations flow.

Our connection is profoundly beautiful.

You remembered me on my birthday every year.

This means the world to me. My eyes shed joyful tears.

I am filled with anticipation and excitement to meet you Friday.

I am elated that we will be together to celebrate Father's Day.

Heartbeat of a Dreamer

Feels as if I am living a dream. I feel intoxicatingly alive.

Dad, this weekend is ours. This is just the beginning.

In my eyes, you are a sparkling gem to be treasured.

I shall love and cherish you always and forever.

Dreams do come true.

My heart has found a home in you.

Dreams do come true.

Beloved Brother

Beloved brother

Beloved brother

Loved and cherished

In darkness you will not perish

Faith rings true in your situation,

Though nights they may be long for you

Angels surround you like a sweet, fragrant perfume.

Beloved brother

Beloved brother

Travesty---a family brought together,

Justice will one day come for you.

Every morning I burn sage for you,

And I pray for you.

Beloved brother

Beloved brother

Chosen child, child of God,

He has a plan for you.

Chosen child, child of God.

Angels are watching over you.

Sweet brother, father, son, and friend

We will wait for you.

We will pray for you.

Beloved brother

Beloved brother

You are a star. Shine on…

Shining brilliant in the golden night sky

I love you, Brother,

My sweet brother

I hope you know how much I love you.

I give thanks for you.

We will wait for you.

Beloved brother

Beloved brother

I Am

I am peace.

I am chaos.

I am fragile.

I am power.

I am a warrior.

I am weak.

I am outspoken.

I am shy.

I am creative.

I am raw.

I am defiant.

I am sweet.

I am a bitch.

I am tame.

I am a dreamer.

I am fragile.

I am strong.

I am still.

I am courage.

I am fear.

I am fearless.

I am beauty.

I am darkness.

I am mystery.

I am fire.

I am a lover.

I am a fighter.

I am stubborn.

I am easy going.

I am moody.

I am still.

I am open.

I am difficult.

I am an artist.

I am reckless.

I am inspiration.

I am pensive.

I am hope.

I am doubt.

I am soft.

I am strong.

I am ordinary.

I am extraordinary.

I am euphoria.

I am melancholy.

I am a flower.

I am a wanderer.

I am a gypsy soul.

Mountain Man

(Inspired by My Father, Jerry)

He feels at peace in wide-open land.

God's country, he says,

"Makes me a happy man."

Where the morning star shines

High in the sky of silken blue

The majestic mountains speak truth.

He puts his heart where blue birds sing,

And finds music in the crisp cool air.

Peace and solitude, he finds here.

In the snowcapped Colorado mountains

The running deer bound through towering pines.

Free among the eagles he longs to fly.

He has hunted for most of his life.

He'll do so until the day he dies.

Mountain man

Far away from city lights

He sleeps beneath the midnight sky.

Mountain man

Heartbeat of a Dreamer

The pale-yellow moon shines on his face
He gazes up at the evening star…and the milky way.
Mountain man
Moved beyond words, a single teardrop falls.
This is home…mother nature calls.
Though she is not always forgiving,
He smiles and says, "Now this is living."
Mountain man
Silent, he listens to the gentle wind blow.
As it rustles the fallen leaves
He's living his dream, one only he knows.
Each morn' he awakes to the auburn sunrise,
A vision of beauty, sweet molasses in the sky
He sits by the fire of dancing flames and glowing embers.
A thousand thoughts rush in--he remembers,
Happy times, years gone by
Beautiful memories to last a lifetime.
Overwhelmed with joy,
He dreams of tomorrow's unknown,
Lost in a world all his own.
Mountain man
Mountain man

I Stand Accused

I call you up to say, "I love you."
Couldn't wait to hear your voice.
But what do you do?
But call me a liar, and say,
"What are you really up to?"
This thing we call love,
Is tainted with pain and accusations.
My soul was filled with fire,
And sheer determination
To win you back,
Regain your adoration.
But day by day, I'm pulling away.
You've pushed me too far,
I don't know who you are.
I stand accused.
Carry on with your words of attack.
Do you think it makes up for all you lack?
You cut me down to size.
No matter what I say, you think it is lies.

Here I sit quiet…as you criticize.

I stand accused.

I don't say a word.

Silent, I glance your way.

I know the truth.

I won't look back, I'll walk away.

I stand accused.

Why do you hang on,

If I am so dirty, low down?

I'm telling the truth,

You think I'm messing around.

Your harsh words ring out in the night.

They ricochet like bullets in flight.

Can't you see?

You are hurting yourself…and me,

With your damn insecurities

The fire in my heart no longer burns for you.

You can blame it on the things you do.

As I turn away, it is you I leave.

I will survive…set me free.

I stand accused.

I stand accused.

Inside My Cage

I live my life day by day inside this cage.

Holding onto forgotten dreams of yesterday

Where love is lost, and hope is locked away within my sorrow.

The auburn sun no longer brings hope for tomorrow.

Memories flood my chaotic mind,

Of life's exquisite dance.

When destiny comes a callin',

Nothing is left to chance.

Always a dreamer---I believed, I believed.

Only now I don't trust---I was deceived.

Inside my cage

I am silent and alone.

Filled with quiet rage.

In my mind, shadows dance on the wall

I sit in the dark, try to make sense of it all.

Inside my cage

Dark spirits of the night whisper and moan

I am truly a wanderer---I don't belong.

Inside my cage

Heartbeat of a Dreamer

A crimson red

I must not bleed.

My shackled soul will not break free.

Inside my cage

The heartache of the past etched deep in my mind

The gentle calm from a storm will never be mine

Passion and love are things I once dreamed of

You and I together---we were intensely alive.

But now you are gone, I am empty inside.

Now I live in solitude.

I have created my own prison cell.

I no longer wish to escape this living hell.

The curtain has closed, as I retreat,

To my cage lined with broken dreams.

Inside my cage

Inside my cage.

Hope, a Smile, and a Prayer

At times, life can feel like a storm.

Heavy black clouds lurk, casting shadows in the moonlight.

Angry, thunderous skies thrash and scream through the night.

Yet a new day dawns, greet it with;

Hope, a smile, and a prayer.

Chances are, what is yet to come is far better than what is gone.

God's ways are mysterious.

From hardship and sorrow, miracles come.

Hope, a smile, and a prayer.

We walk this endlessly long mile,

When the mountain is too steep to climb,

We must pick ourselves up---it is all in the state of mind.

So lovely is the gift of the morning sun.

A red rose in bloom, the grace of the moon

God brings sunshine after a torrential rain.

His rainbows shed light to ease the pain.

Hope, a smile, and a prayer.

The time has come to see diamonds in shattered glass,

Create flames without a match.

Smile through weeping eyes, walk in God's path.

On this journey, we may shed too many tears…

But without sorrow, we could not experience joy.

Without loss, we would not feel love.

Ask for a miracle---be grateful for whatever comes.

Hope, a smile, and a prayer.

Intuition is energy in its purest form.

My spirit flies free, intensely alive,

For I believe…I believe…I believe

Hope, a smile, and a prayer.

We can see pieces of heaven in butterflies in flight.

Birds of song, trees gently swaying in the breeze.

Choose faith over fear and hope over worry.

Live in the moment. Forget the storm's fury.

For every sleepless night, and all the tears we've cried,

God has a blessing in store.

He whispers, "Hold on."

El Baile de la Vida

(The Dance of Life)

Este fuego qué traigo por ti

This fire I bring for you.

Me esta matando por dentro, mi amor

It's killing me inside, my love.

No quiero llorar mas, pues, me duele tanto

Don't wanna cry anymore.

Cuando pienso en tu cara preciosa

When I think of your precious face

No puedo contenerme

I can't…I can't help myself.

Este baile de la vida

Este baile de la vida

In this dance of life, this dance of life

If you choose to dance your dance with someone new

What can I do?

Dance your dance with someone new.

What can I do?

La tristeza que me siento es demasiado

This sadness I feel is just too much.

Mis lagrimas son como perlas qué callen en el mar

My tears are like pearls falling in the sea.

Cuando ciero mis ojos, pues, sueno contigo

Este baile de la vida, este baile de la vida

In this dance of life, in this dance of life

If you choose to dance your dance with someone new

What can I do?

Dance your dance with someone new.

What can I do?

Dance your dance with someone new.

Soulmate

On a crisp fall day, God brought you into my life.

We are meant to be as one,

I am proud to be your wife.

Six years ago; today, we both said, "I do."

We stood hand in hand,

Vowed to love each other in truth.

In a gown of purest lily white

I gazed deep in your steel-blue eyes.

Our bond blessed for eternity,

By God's loving light

Before we met, I often stumbled in blindness.

Not knowing a right turn from wrong

But since we wed,

I've danced on velvet petals of red roses in bloom.

Their intrinsic beauty and my passion for you

Fill my spirit with song.

With each passing year, our love triumphs on

As we follow life's trail,

You are my strength in times of sorrow.

You give me hope for a brighter tomorrow.

You stood beside me as I faced adversity-uncertainty.

You are my courage, my rock, my strength.

When you walk into my arms unreservedly,

I feel a love so pure.

A closeness--a freedom--and peace

An undeniable fire stops my heart's beat.

Over time, all of me has become all of you.

Even when you are not in my presence...

I feel you...

You wash over me like a gentle spring rain,

And my love for you pours.

Now here am I, imperfect...

Yet you look at me through loving eyes.

You accept me, understand me,

Believe in me, love me.

With pen in hand, I tell you how my heart feels.

Words often whispered are never quite clear.

I am reaching out to touch you,

In the way I know how.

My silent vow of devotion

Runs deeply within me.

My sweet love, you are my everything.

When the sun reflects the beauty of your smile

And the gentle breeze whispers your name...

I stop in my tracks. I think of you.

Heartbeat of a Dreamer

In the night sky, the moon shines it's radiant glow.

Distant stars spell out your name.

And I know…I just know,

Our love is a gift offered by God.

I will cherish this gift until death do us part.

You hold the keys to my heart.

Let us walk hand in hand,

In the lavender shadows of the evening

And listen to the songs of twilight birds.

May we follow the stream of laughter,

As we fly among the honey locust trees

Living as two lovers in a dream

A life filled with bliss and togetherness.

You and me

Soulmates…for eternity.

Angels of Healing

Cancer is a word I deplore.

It breeds fear and uncertainty,

Cuts me to the core

But cancer cannot silence courage.

It cannot invade the soul.

Or take away the part of me that God made whole.

Tears flow like a gentle stream,

From the eyes of those who dare to dream

When I feel down,

And the mountain is too steep to climb…

I pick myself up, it's all in the state of mind.

When things go wrong as they sometimes will

The road well-traveled can seem uphill.

On days when I have no song in my heart

I sing anyway.

I have found peace, for life does not end here.

God is my melody. He takes away my fear.

Angels of healing

On your wings I may soar to the sky

If destiny has spoken,

I will choose not to cry.

Thank you to nurses who help us fight this disease,

That devours our strength, brings us to our knees…

But one thing cancer cannot take away is our dignity.

Inner beauty shines from within our souls

With or without hair, our radiance glows.

Angels of healing

With the strength of a thousand warriors sent from above

You nurture our souls with compassion and love.

What can I say about Francie's smiles?

She won her fight, with honor and style.

She is beautiful and brave.

I remember the advice she gave.

"Take it one day at a time, you'll be just fine."

With her words of wisdom, I now live my life.

She has a vision of hope,

To help fellow cancer survivors heal and cope.

Because of her tenacity and drive, the cancer center now thrives.

Angels of healing

Bonnie, you care for me in your sweet, special way.

With kind eyes and a giving heart,

You always know just what to say.

Your golden locks shine in the celestial sun

You make me feel special, like the battle is half won.

Donna, your love for God is perfect and true.

Heartbeat of a Dreamer

When you speak of Him, I listen.

For I love him too.

Eileen, you have the grace of a fine woman.

Your gentle words soothe my soul.

With your encouragement, I can now reach my goal.

Angels of healing

Dr. Lee, you light up the room with your smile and wit.

Your knowledge is remarkable.

Because of you, I will never quit.

You walk in the office like a breath of fresh air.

You open your heart to us, you care.

Of all the weapons we take into battle

Sheer will is the most powerful of all.

Dr. Lee, I hang on to your wise words.

To rise to this challenge and not stumble and fall.

Angels of healing

As winter slowly creeps upon us

Frosty silver nights grow unbearably cold.

In heaven the snow will never chill us

I imagine it is paradise, where we will never grow old.

I take in the great wisdom whispering in the towering pines.

Where all around is still and calm, and my life is still mine

Angels of healing

I want you to know, I will never forget your kind souls.

Each of you has a place etched deep in my heart.

I've learned from your compassion, it's what sets you apart.

I will think of you from time to time,

As I gaze at the glistening moon in the midnight sky

If you listen to the silence echo, you can hear the farthest star cry.

Angels of healing

Time stands still as the pendulum swings.

Let's fill each moment with the promise of what tomorrow brings.

And if tomorrow does not come, give thanks to God, the Almighty One

For love, laughter, and years gone by---with hands raised up to the sky.

Yesterday is just a smile away. Remember the good times---live for today.

To dance the dance in heaven must be like an exquisite dream.

I imagine streets paved with gold, and lush gardens galore.

Exotic flowers in abundance, so much to explore.

Life is a gift of beauty and truth.

Let's grow old with grace--learn from our youth.

Angels of healing

You make us smile.

Sometimes it's nice to forget for a while…

But when times get tough, and the true fight begins,

With our angels of healing

This battle we will win!

Self-Sabotage

Take a good look at yourself.

What are you doing?

You're destroying yourself.

Just who are you fooling?

You don't like yourself.

Someone must have hurt you…

Really hurt you.

It is a free-for-all.

Don't you know what you are doing?

Someone needs to reign you in

Reign you in

You're up all night long.

Can't you see what you're doing…

To yourself, girl?

Nothing will ever…ever be the same.

The time has come to change your ways,

Got to reach out…give it up…give it up.

Don't you long for better days?

Heartbeat of a Dreamer

You are acting crazy, girl.

You deserve so much better,

Then the way you treat yourself.

A Love Letter to God

As I write this letter in the still of the night

Tears of joy fall from my eyes.

The love You give, it amazes me.

Hope keeps me going…You set me free.

I used to walk alone in darkness.

My soul was filled with pain,

My passions unharnessed.

You seemed so far away,

I could barely get through the day.

A love letter to God

You lift me up…

My soul You touch.

Like an eagle, my spirit soars

You keep me longing,

Longing for more

A love letter to God

You are my everything…

With the joy that you bring

I ache for the peace of a warm spring rain.

As drops fall from the sky to ease my shame…

I whisper to You, my innermost feelings.

The pureness of Your love

It sends me reeling.

A love letter to God

You lift me up.

A love letter to God

Heart of Fire and Soul
(Inspired by Carlos Santana)

He has a heart of fire and soul.

The sound of his guitar licks will devour you whole.

He's about peace, love, and light.

Fairness and equality for all

Are his never-ending plight.

His name is Carlos, Carlos Santana

He's talented beyond compare.

He believes in humanity. He truly cares.

He plays with passion like the supersonic

Charge of his guitar.

When you listen to him play…close your eyes

You'll forget who you are.

You'll forget who you are.

He has a heart of fire and soul.

He sets his guitar on fire, playing with desire.

He has a heart of fire and soul

The sound of his guitar echoes

In the brilliant night sky

He will take you on a journey,

Of a natural high

He is humble in his way,

With gentle words to say

With eyes as black as coal

One look from him will pierce your soul

He is an icon, surpassing the semblance of time.

He is in a class all his own.

His music knows no color lines.

He sings about hot mamas,

About their drama.

Important issues in the world,

He brings them to light.

He makes sure they are thought about,

And not hidden out of sight.

He has a gentle soul.

He's smooth. He's calm.

He will forever be loved,

Even after he is gone.

His legacy will live on

His legacy will live on

His name is Carlos, Carlos Santana

His name is Carlos, Carlos Santana

He has a heart of fire…

Why Won't You Look at Me?

Hush…do not say a word. I know it will hurt.

I can see it in your steel--blue eyes,

You want to tell me goodbye.

We sit in silence…

Nothing left to say.

You would walk out that door,

If you had it your way

I try to be strong, fight back the tears.

My heart is pounding…

Filled with nothing but fear.

I'm holding on by a thread,

As our love falls apart

If you still care…do not shatter my heart

Why won't you look at me?

Babe…you're breaking my heart in two.

What can I say? What can I do?

Why won't you look at me?

Please…don't shatter our dreams.

Say something…say anything.

Why won't you look at me?

I do not understand. Why won't you take my hand?

Why won't you touch me…my lover--my friend?

A tear etches a pathway down my cheek.

Don't want to face the harsh reality

As it stares me down…crushes my core

Maybe I just love you more.

I will wait for you to come home…

To open the door

Then I won't feel so all alone

My eyes frantically search yours

For the love I know I am about to lose

You turn away from my gaze.

I feel you…you have gone away.

A thousand thoughts race through my mind

You and me…happier times.

I feel a burning in my eyes.

My heart screams silently for you

I have already lost you…what can I do?

Immeasurable Romance

I am missing you and heaven so greatly.
Our short time was an endless romance.
As we part ways veiled and incognito
The world takes us in no discernable dance.
Do you think of me like I think of you?
I would live in ecstasy if I knew you think of me.
Only lovers can dream all this nonsense away,
Lost in the magic of love for just one more day.
From sunrise to the edge of the moon
I relive every detail of our intimate embrace.
This image is etched deep in my heart,
A sweet cadence that time cannot erase.
Do you think of me like I think of you?
I would live in ecstasy if I knew you think of me.
Only lovers can dream all this nonsense away.
Gripped in the magic for just one more day.
Will I ever breathe the same way again?
My lips miss an occasional passionate kiss.
When we ascend this immeasurable distance

Heartbeat of a Dreamer

To experience emotions, we dare not resist.
Do you think of me like I think of you?
I would live in ecstasy if I knew you think of me.

Mama, in My Eyes

(For My Birth Mother)

Mama, does your soul ache for me?
Was your love so strong, you had to set me free?
When I was a babe, you let me go…said goodbye.
Do you still cry inside?
You were just a girl, running scared.
But I know you loved me…I know you cared.
Mama, do you have a chill in your bones?
Does the torment of the wind leave you feeling alone?
You gave me up, so I would have a better life.
Pure love and sacrifice
You love me in your core, I feel sure of that.
Why don't you search for me?
Mama, where are you at?
Mama, in my eyes…
You are a raven-haired beauty, a lady of grace.
With pain etched deep in your lovely face
Mama, in my eyes…
You are elegant, gentle, refined.

Yet sorrow follows you through the passing of time.
Mama, in my eyes…
You are strong, yet frail like a flower.
You ache for your child lost…
You relinquished your power.
Mama, do you think of me as the seasons change?
In the cold, dead of winter, or the soft summer rain?
Do you lay beneath the canvas of the night sky?
And imagine me shining like a lone star in your mind?
Mama, I pray somewhere in the depth of your soul,
You feel at peace…and somehow you know…
I grew up in a happy, loving home.
I think of you as the years swiftly roll by
I ache for you in the still of the night.
As the clock strikes two, three…four,
I sit in the dark, teardrops fall to the floor.
My dream is that one day our paths will cross,
And you will love me from that day on.

Over the Moon

(In Loving Memory of My Dad, Royce)

I wish upon the brightest star in the night sky.
Get down on my knees and pray,
For more precious time, for one more day
If only we had forever. But forever turned on a dime
Only God knows why He called you home so soon.
When we found each other, you would say with delight,
"I am over the moon! Over the moon!"
My heart dances at the thought of you
Your sweet smile lit up the room.
Filled with the mystery of a thousand stormy skies,
Were your dark, lovely eyes.
I would see a flame ignite when you spoke of happy times.
Dad--- last summer was the greatest of my life.
I, too, was "Over the moon! Over the moon!"
We would talk for hours to pass the time.
You shared your story. I shared mine.
My love for you bloomed like a rose, each day.
I am proud to call you dad.

Heartbeat of a Dreamer

Oh, why did you have to go away?

My soul aches for those lost sunny days,

And our drives to the mountains of Ouray

Strolling hand in hand…together at last

Your visits flew by way too fast.

Today, I am left with memories of unforgettable you.

A smile parts my lips, and once again…

I am "Over the moon! Over the moon!"

I close my eyes and see your smiling face.

I feel your hugs and hear you say,

"I am over the moon! Over the moon!"

I See the Beauty

(For Lovely Gail)

I see the beauty…

In the white morning star

Twinkling like a lone diamond

I see the beauty…

In the distant horizon

A reddish hint of light

Creeps slowly up, in the canopy of the sky

The dawn is the beginning…

Concepts of hope and peace

I see the beauty…

In a rainbow at storm's end

Tranquility rises transcendent,

Transforming thunder into sounds of grace

Light replaces the sky of dark gray.

I see the beauty…

In a garden stroll

Through lavender shadows of the evening

Or the lyrical sound as twilight birds sing.

I see the beauty…

In the luminous night sky's moon

Life is a journey.

A gift of beauty and truth

I see the beauty…

In you

The Silver Rose

She spins like a delicate silver rose.

Silver rose.

Silver rose

One frosty winter night, her petals froze.

Wilting, she dies in the morning sun.

True love lost forever…she feels numb.

Her tender heart turned black.

These is no turning back.

No turning back

Sad, more than sad, she sits with a grieving smile.

Her cries heard across the miles.

The night--speechless, without a soul

The pain she endures, no one knows.

Silver rose

Silver rose

A silver rose, delicate and fine,

With melancholy eyes

With an abandoned spirit, she remains silent in the mist.

Her empty soul of love hesitates to fly free.

Gentle and alone, it finally leaves.

Only her teardrops in the snow remain.

Silent screams cannot wake her from her darkest dream.

Silver rose

Silver rose

She disappears into the velvet black night.

Wandering among towering pines

Lost in time.

Silver rose

Silver rose

So sad, more than sad…

Tears to Triumph

Just last year, my restless heart kept me awake.
Silent stars whispered my name.
The blackness of the night sky made me cry.
Tears fell from my hollow eyes.
"Sweet Jesus…why…why?"
My soul trembled, conquered with fright.
Too frail and weak to hope for the light.
Didn't know if I would live or die.
But the warrior within wanted to fight.
Without strength to rise from bed
Father's words rang true in my head.
"With or without hair, your beauty shines…"
"You are a survivor…God is by your side."
When the mountain was too steep to climb,
Healing hands of light reached down from the sky.
I felt a peace----sweet, sublime.
Strength began to fill my soul…
I no longer felt all alone.
Tears to triumph

Courage and faith

Today, I thrive…by God's grace.

Tears to triumph

I live to tell the tale of a living hell.

The battle is won, my new life has begun.

Tears to triumph

Now I dare to dream.

To ride the wind wherever it takes me.

So lovely is the gift of the morning sun.

A red rose in bloom…the grace of the moon.

God bless all the beautiful warriors,

Who fight this fight with dignity.

We are survivors…we proudly wear pink.

God's Child

(For Devin)

He was just a little boy.

So full of life

He had an old soul,

At the age of five

A fire danced in his eyes,

Sweet handful, wide-eyed child

God's child

Now he is an angel in the sky.

He is home, he wouldn't want us to cry.

God's child

Pure like the winter snow

Gentle like the rain

He brought meaning to life's senseless game.

His spirit glistened in the sun.

He touched our lives, one by one.

God's child

Jesus called him home.

Born to fly free,

Heartbeat of a Dreamer

It was his destiny.

With a precocious mind

He always had to ask why.

He loved to sing, "Great Balls of Fire,"

With a gleam in his eye

He would say, "I am a child of God."

He made the weary smile.

He saved his nickels and dimes,

All the change he could find…

For offering at church on Sunday

He gave his heart every day.

If he comes to you in your dreams

Be at peace, for with the angels he sings.

God's child

God's child

Love Everlasting

(For My Mom, Evelyn)

Mom is such a beautiful word.
The loveliest I have ever heard.
As a babe, you brought me home.
You loved me as your very own.
You laugh my laugh, you shed my tears…
You feel my sorrow, you know my fears.
We dance life's exquisite dance.
Brought together by fate, not by chance.
Your love is made of sacrifice and devotion.
It brings me peace like the crystal-blue ocean.
You knew I must discover the world alone,
Yet your arms welcomed me each time I came home.
I would follow you to the ends of the earth, or the stormy seas.
You have made me who I am, allowed me to fly free.
Your eyes are gentle; they see through me.
Our bond will live on for eternity.
God blessed me with you, my angel, my mom.
We share a deep love. It is a special bond.

Heartbeat of a Dreamer

When all seemed dark and drear

With your precious fire, I felt you were near.

Your strength guides me, gives me wings to fly.

With confidence, I soar like an eagle to the sky.

God made your smile of the sunshine.

Your love for me surpasses the semblance of time.

You are like a beautiful red rose.

With a love for me that only you know.

Side by Side

(Mom and Dad's Sixtieth Wedding Anniversary)

Across the years of yesterday

You pledged your love in a sacred way.

Two golden rings worn proudly to this day,

Symbolize your love so pure.

Your bond is a ray of sun,

A sparkling jewel

You share the wine of sweet togetherness.

Side by side…for sixty years

Nothing compares to the bliss of foreverness.

Love is fragile; love is strong.

It thrives on trust, heart's sweetest song.

Side by side, partners for life

Side by side, as husband and wife

As time rolls by, may you be together till death do you part.

Side by side

Mom, when you have times of sorrow,

Dad walks the extra mile.

With a tender heart, he makes you smile.

He is your rock…strength…your everything.

Side by side

Fill each day with quiet talks on mountain trails.

Towering pines all around you

The sun shining down.

Be still…look around.

You are in God's country.

Feel the beauty of love…of life…of Him.

Listen, as He whispers in the wind,

"Here is the one I have brought to you,"

Let fall a song to echo from the heart,

A faith in deep, abiding, growing love.

Look back on this day and say,

"I shared this with you."

Dream…live…laugh…love.

Side by side

Side by side

Through the Pane of a Frosted Window
(A Christmas Poem)

Through the pane of a frosted window

I watch snowflakes of velvet white fall to the ground.

My spirit filled with love for Jesus…and peace, profound.

The light of our Savior glows and shines

All throughout the year, not just at Christmastime

Jesus brings harmony to my heart.

The melody rings true in my ears.

His loving presence quiets my fears.

In my mind the music lingers

I give thanks as I feel the ivory keys beneath my fingers.

In my dreams, I hear songs of angels.

The dissonance and beauty go hand in hand.

This cold December night, I give thanks for the gift of life.

For red roses in bloom, for the auburn sunrise and whispering pines.

As I follow life's trail, the Lord is my strength in times of sorrow.

He gives me hope for a brighter tomorrow.

He is my courage…strength…grace.

Peace washes over me like a warm spring rain.

Heartbeat of a Dreamer

I dream of walking with him, hand in hand…

We stroll through violet shadows of the evening,

And listen to twilight birds sing.

Tonight, I sit by the fire--watch the flames dance.

By His grace, I am given a second chance.

I gaze at the luminous night sky's moon.

I think of life's journey---a gift of beauty and truth.

Lost in a rhapsody of thought, I drift off to sleep,

And dream a thousand diamond dreams.

I know the beauty of Christmas lives in your heart.

May the everlasting love and light of Jesus,

Bring blessings and peace to you…

This Christmas and always

The Wind in My Soul

Frozen stars refuse to shine…

They have lost their sparkle in this soul of mine

The music of winter is composed in minor keys.

Dissonant chords ricochet off naked birch trees

The wind howls…thunder rolls

Thrashing into my fragile soul

Voices haunt my every waking hour.

Voices taunt me in my dreams.

Spirits of darkness rejoice at my silent screams.

The wind in my soul blows frigid and cold.

My crimson heart has turned to stone.

I feel frightened…alone…with a chill in my bones.

The wind in my soul devours me whole.

I fall to my knees and pray,

"Sweet Jesus, take this hell away."

Tears fall from my troubled, red eyes

"Am I the master of my own demise?"

I hear whispers in the dark,

I see shadows dancing on the wall.

From this quicksand, I cannot crawl.

Demons choke the very breath from me.

Leave me not alone to weep.

Wicked are the ways of the devil…

He laughs wildly in a grand display.

Once intensely alive--I feel dead today.

My soul, shackled in chains…

In agony I remain.

Take me to my grave.

For I may not survive.

Feels like I am buried alive.

A black veil crosses my mind.

Yellow Roses for Sharon

(Gary and Sharon's Love Story)

She passed away on a summer's day.

His love was gone now. On his knees he prayed.

Roses were blooming. The sun was shining.

She would have said, "It's gorgeous here today."

She had a smile to brighten his day,

She always knew just what to say.

He blows her a kiss good night up to the sky,

As he tries, he tries not to cry.

Memories flowing, tears fall like rain…

As he prays her soul to keep

And he drifts off to sleep.

Yellow roses for Sharon

He longed to spend his life with her.

He got down on one knee,

And gave her yellow roses…for eternity…

For eternity

Yellow roses for Sharon

They would grow old together.

With love in their eyes

Their love would last forever…forever.

Yellow roses for Sharon

Yellow roses for Sharon

What Can I Do?

Just sittin' alone at my piano

This house just ain't no home

He's distant—far away.

We sit together with nothing left to say.

Babe, when we found each other,

I never dreamed we'd be this way…but…still…

What can I do?

What can I do?

Don't know where to turn,

Can't seem to talk to you…anymore.

I can't stand the silence…

Is it time for me to find the door?

I don't want to leave you. I'm so confused.

Babe, I'll never get over you…no…no…no

What can I do?

What can I do?

This Poem: My Gift

(For My Mom, Evelyn)

Scenes from my window…

Flash before my eyes.

I admire the beauty of the ice-blue sky.

Autumn leaves fall, as auburn trees gently sway.

The sun shines bright on this November day.

Scenes from my soul…

Move me beyond words

Your smile, so lovely, unforgettable and pure

You are the light of my life.

Being with you, I feel vibrant…alive.

Scenes of celebration…

A day to be cherished.

Mom, your eightieth birthday is a blessing, a gift.

My heart is filled with joy—my spirit's uplifted.

Scenes from the sea…

Waves roll out to meet the setting sun.

Vibrant colors splatter the canvas in the sky.

I think of you, Mom—tears fill my eyes.

I am so thankful for your devotion and sacrifice.

For us, you would lay down your life.

Scenes with our family…

I reminisce, I remember,

All the happy times we have shared.

We know you love deeply. You show that you care.

I smile, as I think of good times to come,

Togetherness, laughter, our family as one.

Scenes from the future…

God bless you, Mom.

May joy fill your heart as years roll by

Always know you are cherished…

Dear light of my life

Scenes from heaven…

I will forever love you.

We share a bond, sacred and true.

When God calls, and it is your time to go.

I will feel sad, and yes, I will cry,

But I'll feel your presence…always close.

You will be with me wherever I go.

Peaceful as a gentle breeze

Your love light will carry me.

On your eightieth birthday…

This poem is my gift.

God gives me the words,

That flow from my lips.

With pen in hand,

I pour out my soul.

I cherish you.

I love you, Mom.

Hollywood to Hops

I never thought I could, but I did.
You don't know what you can do, what's inside
Till you're in a place, you never thought you'd reside.
I used to be in Napa, tastin' all the wines.
Fancy and free, it was sublime.
Now I'm in Olathe, twistin' up the vines.
Instead of walking down Rodeo
Goin' through the shops
I'm on a farm, working in these hops.
I get to see them grow. I get to see them thrive.
It's more rewarding than a ninety-minute drive.
From Hollywood to hops
It's beyond expression.
The work never stops.
My days are spent in sunshine,
I feel its warmth every day.
Dragonflies circle around me
As if they have a story to tell.
Can't wait to harvest, to see them in a beer.

Taste the hops I grew, appreciate our brew.

The red carpet was fun.

The parties were a ball.

Tastin' my hops is the biggest blast of all.

I've got my headphones on

I'm jammin' to my favorite song.

Sittin' bumper to bumper is a thing of the past.

I'm sittin' on my mower having a blast.

From Hollywood to hops

From plastic to paradise

It's beyond my wildest imagination.

After a long day in the sun,

I'm sippin' on a cold one,

My work is finally done.

From Hollywood to hops

From Hollywood to hops

No Color Lines

We have a choice to make.
It's time to love, not discriminate.
Why walk through life with a shackled soul?
Let freedom reign. It can make us whole.
"When will we find a way to love?"
I ask this question to the Lord above.
It's all about unity. It should be about trust.
So, what if he is white or black?
Why should the black man fall under attack?
God is watching. He sees all.
Why should the black man take the fall?
We cause our mothers so much pain.
She cries all night. Is her boy all right?
This is life. It is not a game.
Of how dirty we can play
We ought to feel ashamed.
Children join gangs just to fit in
Forced to commit unimaginable sins.
No color lines.

It's time for a change.

It's time. It's time.

Don't change your mind from doing the

Right thing

Because you're afraid of what

The neighbors might think.

What if a white girl falls in love

With a black man?

What is it about love we don't understand?

No color lines.

It's time for a change.

No color lines.

Mile-High Sundays

Have you ever heard about Sundays at
Mile-High?
Fans cheer. The noise reaches to the sky.
The sun shines. Fans work on their tans.
We love the Broncos as only a true fan can.
Manning has a ninety-five-million dollar arm.
The opposing defense, he disarms.
His plays are illusion, mass confusion.
Sit in the sunshine. Have another beer.
Sit in the stands. Join in on the cheers.
When the Thomas boys catch the ball
And score
They leave us Bronco fans longing for more.
Elway's on board. The Broncos just scored.
It's so exciting, you'll never get bored.
Mile-High Sundays
Come have a blast.
It's even better than I remember,
Better than years past

Heartbeat of a Dreamer

Mile-High Sundays
Will we be Super Bowl bound?
They say we're the best team around.
I remember watching Elway,
With one of his famous fourth-quarter drives
He is clearly the best quarterback alive.
The Super Bowl against Green Bay
I remember it like it was yesterday.
Elway threw long to Shannon Sharpe.
Oh, what a team. They played with such heart.
The Three Amigos scored many a touchdown.
They were the best damn receivers in town!
I remember the Orange Crush.
I loved them so much.
Chavous, Moses, Alzado, and Gradishar
They made you forget all of your problems.
Made you forget who you are.
We hated the Raiders. We do to this day.
We crush them. We make them pay.
I loved to watch Upchurch run the ball back.
He blew past the defense. Never got sacked.
So come on down to Bronco land.
Watch the game, drink a beer,
Be a Bronco fan.
Mile-High Sundays
Mile-High Sundays

Who Are "They"?

He said, she said, who said, they said…

The so-called experts say.

Well, who are they anyway?

Undeniable arrogance, they reach for the sky,

They have an opinion, but they don't know why.

They live in glass houses. They throw stones.

One day they're going to wake up all alone.

Who are "they"?

They report the evening news,

It's giving me the blues.

Their heads are buried in the clouds,

Yes, you really said that out loud.

They talk about freedom,

It changes with the seasons.

Well, who are "they"?

They'll turn on a dime,

They'll do it to you every time.

Who are "they"?

Who are "they"?

He's a Happy Man

He's my brother.

I love him as only a sister can.

He is a courageous man.

He amazes me.

He has a heart of gold.

He loves the young

He loves the old

He's a happy man.

He's a father.

He's a son.

He is a chosen one.

He loves the Lord

He has faith in mankind.

He sees only the good

As we all should.

He's not proud; he is humble.

Through his life he has surely stumbled.

He picks himself up.

He never gives up.

He's not selfish; he's pure.

As he walks through fire

Love of his family is all he desires.

As he walks through darkness

He looks at me and says,

"I'm a happy man."

"I'm a happy man."

The Winter Rose

As winter slowly creeps in
Frosty silver nights grow cold.
There was but one red rose left
On a blanket of snow.
The crisp autumn air has grown too cold to bear.
A lover leaves his beloved beauty to dance
With someone he has yet to meet.
Maybe she will appear as a vision
Of grace in his dreams.
As the seasons changed,
He grew distant.
Now a stranger to the winter rose
His icy stares were too much to bear.
Her petals froze
The pain she endures, only she knows
He left without goodbyes
Leaving her soul lost
Salty teardrops to fall.
She is the winter rose

Slowly wilting in the snow

But the strong survive

Maybe one day, this he will know.

The winter rose

Alone, she stands…

Her beauty and allure fade.

She waits for the return of her man

With each passing day

Yet he is ripe with desire

For a lover to star in his dreams.

Maybe they will cross paths

Like two souls in flight

His eyes are filled with fire for her

While the winter rose waits…

For her dream to come to fruition

She has not listened to her inner voice…

Her intuition.

For this man has left a trail of tears behind

Her wounded crimson heart will bleed

Until the end of time.

The winter rose

The winter rose

Smoke and Mirrors

Exhilarating nights on the red carpet
Can feel like a dream
It is all an illusion
Nothing is as it seems
One day you will wake up
Get a reality check
It won't be pretty
Guess that's life in the big bad city
Smoke and mirrors
You're not the center of the universe
Your beauty is both a blessing and a curse
You hope someone will see through your veil of tears
You have been searching for love year after year
Smoke and mirrors
It is all going to come to an end one day
You are like a character in a one-act play
You will do anything to get your big break
You have lost your identity in the land of the fake
As you drive by the Hollywood sign

Heartbeat of a Dreamer

You are lost in thought about the good old times
Nights strolling down the Sunset strip
With the cool, the beautiful, and the hip
Every Joe producer around…
Has heard about the new kid in town.

Break Up

We love each other

Why can't we just get along?

We hate each other

Why won't we simply say

When we are wrong?

Last night we had another fight

He said, she said…

We both think we're right

Why don't we break up?

Just so we can make up

It sounds like so much fun

I always leave and then,

I come running back

Running back…

For more.

I Dance with God

Though I have danced a thousand dances
And cried for second chances,
I always run to His sweet embrace.
I long for His compassion, His grace.
God inspires me endlessly
My spirit soars, He sets me free.
I thought I had seen it all over the years,
Only to shed salty primal tears.
But as circumstances changed,
I finally found my way.
Out of the dark and into the light
I whispered His name in the silent, still night
And now…
I dance with God
I dance a different life
I dance with God
Through hard times and strife
I dance with God
He changed my nights

To the brightest of days.

I dance with God

At the stars in His eyes, I gaze

He is my strength when I am weak

When I turn a blind eye…He sees for me

He picks me up when I stumble and fall

He's all knowing, loves me through it all.

Seasons come, and they go

How times have changed.

With the exception of God's love,

Nothing stays the same.

As winter slowly turns to spring

I don't worry about what tomorrow brings

Because for God, my soul forever sings

He is my best friend; He is my everything.

I dance with God

I feel his peace

His presence surrounds me

O, to be with Him for eternity

I dance with God

I can never thank Him enough

For his understanding and love

I dance with God

Glory to heaven above

I dance with God

I dance with God

Brown-Eyed Boy

Elijah, the beauty of your name could not compare

To the beauty of your angelic face.

Nor will there ever be another who could take your place.

Brown-eyed boy

You left behind the echo of your smile, to shine brighter

Then the perfect stars floating in the night sky.

A work of art…a masterpiece of bravery.

God created you to have the strength of a thousand warriors.

To be a hero, a son, a brother. A gentle boy with

Grace and valor like no other.

Brown-eyed boy

Your childhood was lost on the battlefield of life.

Yet through it all, you smiled that sunshine smile.

Your suffering could not silence your courage

Or dampen your soul.

Or take away the part of you that God made whole

Brown-eyed boy

Let your spirit fly free, run with the wind.

Stroll with Jesus hand in hand.

Heartbeat of a Dreamer

Let your laughter linger in the breeze,
Filling your dad's dreams.
Brown-eyed boy
You came into your mom and dad's life by God's grace,
Not by chance.
The years you had together were a gift,
Like a rainbow at storm's end.
Jason and Carrie, as husband and wife, you walk side by side.
In the scrapbook of life, cherish your memories,
And make new ones.
Fill each page with quiet talks…walks on mountain trails,
Whispering pines abound. As the noonday sun shines down…
Feel the beauty of love…of life…of Him.
Brown-eyed boy
You bloom like a flower in heaven, of velvet petals white.
Jesus has called you home to His kingdom in the sky.
Never to wilt in the sun, never to grow cold on frosty winter nights.
For heaven is paradise.
Dance with angels. No more pain, no more strife.
Now your heart is filled with joy. You feel vibrant, alive.
A flame dances in your eyes.
Brown-eyed boy
At times, a deafening silence echoes in the still of the night…
For those you left behind.
May peace fall over their hearts as they wait for the sun to rise
Like sweet molasses in the sky.

May your family see your smile in the clouds rolling by.

This is just, "So long."

Not goodbye

My Brother…My Inspiration

My brother…my inspiration

It is your birthday, that's cause for celebration

Although you may be amid difficult times

The light of Jesus shines down upon your face

He blesses you with extraordinary grace

Rest in the comfort of His presence

Remember that nothing is impossible.

Dream, my brother, dream…

Of happy times to come with your family.

You will feel fantastically free.

You inspire me with your courage, strength, and grace.

God is with you; keep on keeping the faith.

Walk step-by-step through this journey of life,

Hand in hand with the Lord through struggle and strife.

I believe in miracles. I believe in you.

I trust in God. He will never forsake you.

You are God's child.

You are a beautiful, kind man.

For your future, He has a plan.

Heartbeat of a Dreamer

My brother…my inspiration…

Reflect on visions of paradise

Where pure joy and love withstand the test of time.

Close your eyes, envision the crystal-blue water in Ridgeway.

Imagine yourself, with your feet gently splashing.

You bask in the warmth of the noonday sun,

And dream of happy times to come.

God made the morning star

To shine in the sky of silken blue.

He has such love in his heart for you.

God made the birds to sing a sweet melody in spring.

He filled the world with beauty and joy…

He did that for you.

Follow him to rainbows' end

Walk and talk with Him—your closest friend.

My brother…my inspiration

My birthday wish for you will most surely come true.

May you have a blessed year, filled with joy in your heart,

And with each passing year, may you find hope for tomorrow.

May you soar like an eagle in the ice-blue sky.

I pray for the miracle of your presence

To be with us, what a gift from heaven!

So-- dream, my brother, dream

You are everything to me.

I look up to you and admire you from afar.

As I gaze at the night sky and wish upon a distant star,

I wish to be with you again, my brother, my friend.

You are my perpetual song.

When I think of you, the hours fly by

And time stands still

A sweet melody dances in my mind.

Memories of you make me smile.

My brother…my inspiration

God's rainbow is a beautiful sight

Like a shooting star, on a starry night.

A band of colors in hues so soft

Lovely pastels in nature's loft

At the end of the rainbow,

There is a pot of gold.

My brother, *you* are my rainbow,

My pot of gold

Warm, spring days need sunshine, like the sunshine *you* are.

For you shine brighter than the most beautiful morning star.

And the warmth that your sunshine brings to me

My brother, my inspiration,

Dream…

Dream…

Dream…

Hechizado (Spellbound)

Quien eres tu, hombre qué me intriga asi?

Who are you, man that intrigues me so?

Me quedo con los ojos ansiosos, de lo qué

Mi corazon ya sabe.

I stare with eager eyes at what my heart already knows.

Te siguere dondequiera qué sopla el viento.

I'd follow you wherever the wind blows,

Te has lanzado un hechizo

You cast one hell of a spell on me.

Hombre fascinante me cautivar

Mesmerizing man, you captivate me.

Te quiero, me quieres a mi?

I want you…do you want me?

Me dejas hechizado…hechizado

Me dejas hechizado…hechizado.

You leave me spellbound…

Spellbound.

La magia en tus ojos persiste en mi mente.

The magic in your eyes lingers in my mind.

Secudes mi mundo una y otra vez.

You rock my world, time after time.

Me siento hypnotizada

I feel hypnotized.

Sueno contigo, amante de fantasia

I dream of you, fantasy lover.

Come to me in the night undercover

You cast one hell of a spell on me.

Me dejas hechizado…hechizado.

Me dejas hechizado…hechisado.

You leave me spellbound…

Spellbound.

Torn

Do you think of me when you drift off to sleep?

I wonder if you'll soon forget…

Will you remember me?

I am reeling from the scorching hot day

When we said goodbye, babe.

I'll love you until the day I die.

At times, I feel close to you,

Like no one else matters.

Yet tonight when we spoke,

You seemed distant, far away.

Is there someone else occupying your mind?

Is she there with you now?

Is she there all the time?

I'm torn

I still love you

I'm torn

I ache for your touch

I'm torn

Didn't know I could hurt so much

I'm torn

Will we find a way to be together again?

I'm torn

I miss you, my lover, my friend

I'm torn

Do you mean the sweet words you say?

I'm torn

Or do you just love me for now, for today.

Don't know what tomorrow will bring

Will my heart cry for you?

Or will it sing?

This frigid January night,

I look back on happier times

Sorrow hasn't faded, not in the least

In fact, the pain I feel brings me to my knees

I pray to God to show me the way

Should I walk this path alone?

Can't bear the thought,

I miss you, babe,

You are my home.

Whatever happens over time

In my heart, you will always be mine

Please know my love for you is true

You are my soulmate.

I only want you.

I'll never love like this again

I'll look for you in heaven

Our love will live on for eternity,

It will never end.

Torn…

Torn…

A Poem for Shea

Shea,

You shine like a sapphire in the vast sky

Your playful spirit, free as a butterfly

Dancing around…barefoot…carefree dove

You embody joy, peace, light, love.

Pools of crystal fire flicker in your eyes

You are joy at its finest.

In love with living, through the eyes of a child,

Your smile…a ray of sunshine on a cloudy day.

As the sun went down on yesterday eve…

Setting like sweet honey in the sky,

You and I played the piano and sang.

You made me smile.

I made a note to myself,

"Never lose your inner child."

As I listened to your melodies flow from your lips

You felt the ivory keys beneath your fingertips.

The autumn sky slowly turned dark,

As stars appeared, in all their luster.

Heartbeat of a Dreamer

One by one…in the night…velvet…speechless

Shea,

You are a delightful and sweet girl,

Floating on a ray of sunshine.

You are giving and patient,

With the grace of a fine young girl.

You fill my home with laughter and light

A heartfelt thank-you for a fantastically fun night!

God has blessed you with many gifts…

A beautiful heart, and playful nature.

A loving family…and songs that live in you.

Listen to your heart. Understand how it feels

When it puts a pen to paper and writes music

To stir the soul.

XOXOXO

You Brighten My World

I adore your exquisite face

The way your blue eyes twinkle in the noonday sun.

I feel loved, I know I am the only one

I prayed to God for a man of honor,

To cherish till death do us part.

You are my gift, you are my song

You are my everything,

You stole my heart.

I wonder, sometimes, if you realize

How I melt in your presence

Just to know you are mine.

Your touch…your fire

Brings me to my knees.

Two hearts intertwined

I am yours, and you are mine.

The flame of our love

Will never lose its allure.

Our bond is timeless and pure

You brighten my world

I want to be your forever girl.

You brighten my world

You bring sunshine with your smile.

For me, you would walk the longest mile.

We are in this together…till the end,

As husband and wife, lovers, best friends.

You are part of me, always will be.

You are my warrior, my strength, when I am weak.

You calm my spirit when I have had enough.

Don't have to pretend I can take it.

Don't have to be tough.

I will wait for you until time stands still…

Even longer…you know I will.

Babe, I'd lay down my life for you.

I know you would do the same for me too.

I fall deeper in love with each passing year

I trust you. Our bond has cast out all fears.

Sweet love, if tomorrow was our last day

I would not cry. I'd give thanks for today,

For you are by my side…my joy…my light.

I will stand by you. I will never run.

For you are the only one.

You brighten my world

You brighten my world.

You Are...to Me

You are...to me, an inspiration.

Your energy brings peace...tranquility.

Gracious, gentle, strong,

Your spirit is like music of the universe

Ringing true in my ears.

I have not forgotten your smile over the years.

As I reflect on days gone by...

I still hear your loving words...sometimes unspoken,

Expressed through your gentle brown eyes.

The night we met...I felt a beauty profound.

Warm was my spirit...there was peace all around.

I stared with eager eyes at what my heart already knew...

It had found another heart...a place to call home,

A sense of peace...a kindred spirit.

My heart just knew...

To this day, you touch my soul from afar,

You light up the sapphire sky, like a magnificent star.

You are...to me

A soft, glowing sunset...a sea of crystal blue.

Heartbeat of a Dreamer

A full moon…an auburn sunrise…is what I wish for you.

You lifted me up through times of sorrow,

When I had lost hope for a brighter tomorrow.

You accepted me…with all my flaws

When I walked alone in darkness…

My spirit, broken and raw

I could not find shelter from the cold, damp rain,

Didn't know how to overcome the pain.

You dried my tears…yet I still searched

Not realizing you were near.

Your presence will forever dance in my mind

What sweet memories to enchant

Withstanding the semblance of time.

The purity of your heart, so giving…forever true

You are…unforgettable

You are…to me.

Black Blood

Black blood courses through my veins

Veiled and incognito, I smile to hide the pain

Crumpled and stained pages taint my creations.

Robbing my works of their last drop of beauty.

Dripping from the open wound I call my soul,

Are dark spirits of the night,

They devour me whole.

Fanciful flights cut like a knife

When my cold empty reality

Lies naked before my eyes.

With an unquiet mind,

I venture through life,

Vacillating between melancholic lows

And fervent highs.

Black blood

Coming to the aftermath of a storm

I am not the same woman I was when I walked in.

Complicated and moody,

I try to absorb each sensation,

And allow it to move through me…

Depleting me of every ounce of energy.

I am broken and at times, difficult to love.

Longing to come out of the dark…

But sinking in quicksand,

I fight to break free.

I must, once again, pick up my sword

And get ready for battle.

Today, I am a warrior

Tomorrow, I will feel weak,

Crawling on my knees…

No one to hear my silent screams.

Black blood

Black blood

You're My Everything

All I do is think of you, from the sunrise to the edge of the moon.

As I lay awake in your arms,

Stars shine down from the canvas in the sky,

Illuminating the fire in your eyes

I can't hear myself think.

Your soul speaks to me, as I watch you sleep.

You look so peaceful now.

Is it my face you see in your dreams?

Is it my face you see in our jeweled reality?

Unity, we are like two flames ignited.

We have become one.

What I see in your eyes is a fire burning bright

With emotion and desire.

We celebrate our love today.

God, I give thanks for the man of my dreams,

You're my everything…

My everything.

You are my best friend. Our love will never end.

You are my strength.

You lift me up when I am weak.

No words can describe how much you mean to me.

You're my everything

My everything.

You are the clouds floating in the vast sky.

The crimson sunset that brings tears to my eyes.

You are my treasure until the day I die.

I will be your loving wife.

God bless the road that led us here.

You're my everything…

My everything.

Miss Jet Set

She's cruisin' through life

Not a care in the world.

She's an uptown girl.

From Madrid to London and off to Rome

The world has become her home.

She likes crystal and caviar

She likes Dom Perignon

She's wild about discotheques and the bars.

Careful, girl, don't you take it too far.

Miss Jet Set

Up all night, hasn't slept yet.

Miss Jet Set

She likes the pretty boys

They are her toys

Miss Jet Set

One day, you're going to get burned.

Maybe, then you will learn.

Vegas is her playground

She loves roulette

She's waiting for Mr. Right

He hasn't shown up yet.

She flirts with the captain as she boards the plane

She has a drink or two…

Feelin' no pain.

But deep inside, she feels alone.

The world is not any kind of home.

Miss Jet Set

Miss Jet Set

In My Eyes

(For My Dad, Jerry)

There is an opening in my heart

Where only you can go

So deep and rooted in my soul,

That you are my perpetual song.

My love for you courses through my veins…

A reminder of the bond we share, again and again.

I have a raindrop.

I sprinkle it with love.

I wrap my arms around you,

And thank the Lord above.

In my eyes

You are my perfect snowflake

On winter's endless white.

You are my single daffodil in May

Standing tall and proud in the sunlight…

You bring me such delight.

In my eyes,

You are like a rose with petals

Shaped to form a smile.

For me, Dad, you have walked the extra mile.

When I shed a tear,

And it is streaming down my face

With a smile and wise words,

You make it go away.

In my eyes,

You are music of the galaxies

Roaring in my ears.

The promise of the heavens,

Quiets all my fears.

Your love gives me a sense of what I can become

My unbound potential is bound

By your unconditional love.

Mafia Man

Took a vacation down to Mexico

What was in store for me, I didn't know.

Distinguished in his pinstriped suit,

He was fancy, how'd he make all that loot?

He was a real smooth talker…

Man, did he have a line,

"Hey, beautiful lady, how about a glass of wine?"

Mafia man

Tall, dark, and tan

Mafia man

He owned the south of the border…

All that land.

Mafia man

He was a snake in the grass

Told me I was full of sass

Mafia man

He had power. He was filthy rich.

Mafia man

He didn't know I could be such a bitch.

I woke up to his goons banging on my door.

They grabbed me and my luggage,

Tossed me out the door.

They took me to the limo,

With two following behind.

I knew I was in danger

This seems to happen from time to time.

I made my great escape

I flung open the door and ran away

I heard one of his goons say,

"He'll find you one day."

With eyes black as coal, he said,

"You made me look like a fool."

"You're out of line, that just ain't cool."

Haunting Eyes

I walk past the mirror,
Taken aback by what I see.
Eyes dark, sorrowful…empty
Staring back at me.
I fight like a warrior.
On the battlefield, I stand tall.
But I am tired and weary
I don't feel strong at all.
Haunting eyes
They pierce the very depths of my soul
Almost black as midnight
Breast cancer has taken its toll.
Am I a fallen angel from the vast sky?
Am I lost, left to wander alone in the dark?
Haunting eyes
Now lacking hope
I am painfully aware that I cannot cope.
I fall to my knees and pray,
"God, give me strength today."

Heartbeat of a Dreamer

I look at the girl in the mirror.

She is overcome with fear.

A single tear trickles down my face.

Haunting eyes

Serve as a reminder

That time stands still for no one.

Although I feel lost and fearful…

I know in my heart,

That I will live, laugh, and love again.

The day will come when this too shall pass

I feel the light of Jesus shine down on me

I find peace in that for my life,

God has a plan.

He will hold me up with His righteous right hand.

I'll Leave the Porch Light Burnin'

I'll leave the porch light burnin' for you, babe

Hopin' you'll stop by this evening.

I've got somethin' special in mind.

Can you be here in five?

You see, I'm crazy, crazy for your love.

I can't get enough.

Wrap me up in your arms, hold me tight

Tell me, tell me, "I've got you."

About you, boy, I wouldn't change a thing.

Oh…by the way…you're lookin' good in those jeans.

I'll leave the porch light burnin' tonight.

When I'm with you, my spirit flies.

The magic of your smile lingers in my mind.

I'll leave the porch light burnin' tonight.

You've captured my heart…you hold the key.

You stare into my soul…with hunger in your eyes.

Passion's flame ignites, illuminating the sky.

Our love is real…feels good…feels right.

I'll leave the porch light burnin' tonight.

Heartbeat of a Dreamer

I close my eyes, feel your touch,

Never wanted anyone this much.

Before me, you stand, the man I adore

You leave me wantin' more.

Lost in this moment with my lover, my friend…

I have you now, but I hope this never ends.

I don't underestimate the power of our connection,

You are the object of my affection.

Take me by the hand…to dance our dance.

Our paths crossed. It wasn't by chance.

When you walk into my arms unreservedly,

A fire stops the beat of my heart.

Distant stars spell out your name,

I breathe you in…my twin flame.

I'll leave the porch light burnin'

I'll leave the porch light burnin'

Sea of Love

My hand brushes the waves of your love for the thousandth time.
I hold you in my heart this dark, lovely night.
Whispering waters envelop our souls,
With a passion so intense, it devours us whole.
As the moonlight flickers on the crystal-blue sea,
I am safe in your arms, where I long to be.
Tumultuous waves plunge us into the deep,
Where we hold our dreams of tomorrow.
Together as one, we are at peace.
From the edge of the moon to the auburn sunrise
Our primal desire melts on white summer sands
The water of the sea opens its hands.
In this exquisite dance of life,
I am proud to be with you.
Our sea of love is real, it is true.
You belong with me; I belong with you.

Manic

Her moods—they change like the seasons.

Spring or fall, she doesn't need a reason.

Happy one minute and crying the next,

She descends into madness.

Her days and nights are filled with anguish,

Profound sadness.

She cannot mask the pain…anymore.

She runs wildly into the night…

It is a living hell…

A living hell.

Manic

She is wide awake

Manic

Can't you hear her silent screams?

Panic

Nowhere to hide

Panic

She's on one hell of a ride.

Darkness…deep despair

The nightmare never ends.

Torment is her only friend.

Manic…panic…manic…panic

Forever

To know him is to love him.
There are so many things…
I could go on and on.
He is the man of my dreams.
But somehow, as the years passed swiftly by
Our joy turned to sorrow,
Without hope for tomorrow.
I cried myself to sleep every night.
Lying in bed with a stranger by my side.
The day came when I ran away.
I couldn't take it yet another day.
Solitude became my long-lost friend,
Memories of him haunting me to the bitter end.
Slowly our wounds began to heal.
We spoke gentler words for hours it seemed.
Each night, looking forward to our talks and quiet walks
Forever
This love of ours will last
Never mind the pain of our past.

Forever

No matter what tomorrow may bring,

He will always be the one for me.

Forever

Whether apart or together,

I believe that things will get better.

Forever

Our bond will live on,

He is my sweetest melody, my song.

Forever

I can't imagine a day without him.

I don't feel he will ever leave.

He doesn't abandon those he loves.

He is a man of his word…

He is true to me.

Exposed

I should have drowned long ago.

Ocean waves pull me down…down…down.

The rawness of mania leaves me utterly exposed.

I have no skin.

I feel madness rising within.

Wickedness fills the space around me.

Shadows slowly dance on the wall.

I feel as though I am descending into hell.

Exposed…utterly…undeniably…exposed.

Hold onto the Fire

Draw me close, pull me in to your embrace.

I look in your eyes, whisper your name.

I say softly, "Hold onto the fire…hold on."

I feel the throbbing of our hearts

They beat as one.

But will time apart break our impenetrable bond?

We lay in each other's arms

Silent, lost in thought.

We listen to our favorite country song.

Takes us back to happier times.

Nights of bliss…when your lips softly brushed mine,

In a lingering kiss.

Hold onto the fire…hold on.

Hold onto the fire…hold on.

Salty teardrops fall from our eyes,

Like a soft rain falling from the sky…

Plucked from the vapors of our cries.

We used to dance in the moonlight,

As if for the very first time.

Heartbeat of a Dreamer

We would talk and laugh all night.

Heartbeats synchronized.

If I could go back in time…

I would build a bridge to span the miles between us.

I miss our love, uninhibited and free,

When we were meant to be.

I'd sell my soul to see that smile…

A smile only meant for me.

Babe, can we get it back?

Or should we just let it be?

Hold onto the fire…hold on.

Hold on to the fire…hold on.

Don't let the flame flicker out.

Hold onto our connection

Raw…and true.

Your heart belongs to me,

And mine to you.

Hold onto the fire…hold on.

Hold onto the fire…hold on.

Tonight, you told me

Whether we are together forever or not

I will always and forever be your girl.

Then why do I feel as if

This is the end of my world?

My kingdom is about to crumble to the ground,

I feel the tears rollin' down.

Heartbeat of a Dreamer

I guess we have come to a crossroads.

Neither of us knows if we should stay

Or walk away.

But, babe…I still ache for you

With the ardor of my blood.

www.ingramcontent.com/pod-product-compliance
Ingram Content Group UK Ltd.
Pitfield, Milton Keynes, MK11 3LW, UK
UKHW022239230426
12048UKWH00018BA/1361